Incredible Insects

Claire Llewellyn

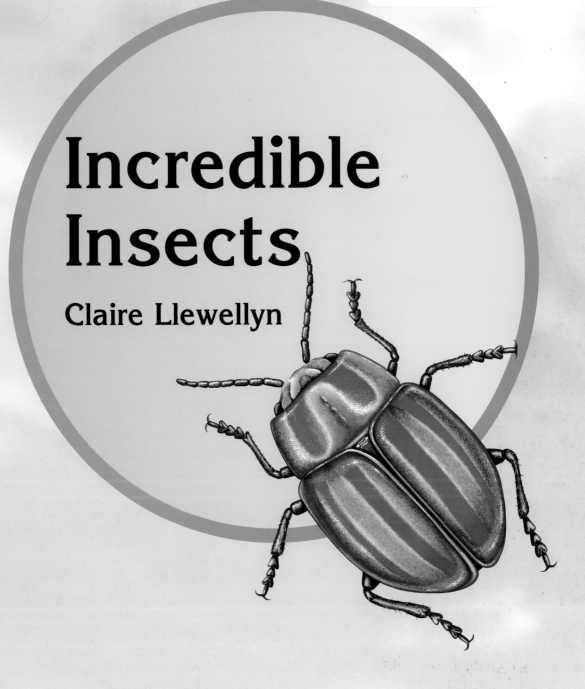

Heinemann Educational Publishers
Halley Court, Jordan Hill, Oxford OX2 8EJ
a division of Reed Educational & Professional Publishing Limited
www.heinemann.co.uk

Heinemann is a registered trademark of
Reed Educational & Professional Publishing Limited

First published 2000
Original edition © Claire Llewellyn 1998
Literacy World Satellites edition © Claire Llewellyn 2000
Additional writing for Satellites edition by Wendy Cobb

07
10 9 8 7 6

ISBN 978 0 435118 93 8 *LW Satellites Incredible Insects* single copy
ISBN 978 0 435118 97 6 *LW Satellites Incredible Insects* 6 copy pack

Designed by M2
Printed and bound in China by CTPS

Acknowledgements
Photos   Andy Purcell / Bruce Coleman Ltd, page 5 top. P. Morris /
Ardea London Ltd, page 5 bottom. Ardea London Ltd, page 7. Kjell
Sandved / Oxford Scientific Films, page 9. Jane Burton / Bruce
Coleman Ltd, page 10 top. John Clegg / Ardea London Ltd, page 10
bottom. Peter Steyn / Ardea London Ltd, page 11. Daniel Heuchlin /
NHPA, page 15. M.P.L Fogden / Bruce Coleman Ltd, page 16. Gerald
Cubitt / Bruce Coleman Ltd, page 17 top. Andrew J. Purcell / Bruce Coleman Ltd,
page 17 bottom. Claudio Nuridsany and Marie Perennou / Science Photo Library, page 20 top.
Alastair Macewen / Oxford Scientific Films, page 20 bottom and page 21 middle. Peter Parks / Oxford
Scientific Films, page 21 top. London Scientific Films, page 21 bottom.

Illustrations / Mark Stewart (Wildlife Art Agency), title page and page 4. Roger Goringe (Garden Studio),
contents page right and top, pages 6, 7, 9, 11 ,18 and 20. Mike Atkinson (Garden Studio), contents page left,
imprint page bottom, pages 12 (except top left), 13 (except top left) and 21. John Butler (Ian Fleming and
Associates), imprint page top and page 8. Alan Male (Linden Artists), pages 12 top left, 13 top left, 14, 15
and 19. David Wright (Kathy Jakeman Illustration), pages 16 and 17.

Also available at Stage 1 of *Literacy World Satellites*

ISBN 978 0 435118 91 4 *LW Satellites: The Search for Tutankhamen* single copy
ISBN 978 0 435118 95 2 *LW Satellites: The Search for Tutankhamen* 6 copy pack

ISBN 978 0 435118 92 1 *LW Satellites: Making the Past into Presents* single copy
ISBN 978 0 435118 96 9 *LW Satellites: Making the Past into Presents* 6 copy pack

ISBN 978 0 435118 94 5 *LW Satellites: How a Book is Made* single copy
ISBN 978 0 435118 98 3 *LW Satellites: How a Book is Made* 6 copy pack

ISBN 978 0 435119 00 3 *LW Satellites: Teacher's Guide Stage 1*
ISBN 978 0 435118 99 0 *LW Satellites: Guided Reading Cards Stage 1*

Contents

What is an insect?   4

Insect families   6

Wings   8

Insect senses   10

Growing up   12

Feeding   14

Staying alive   16

Living together   18

Insects in the home   20

Glossary   22

Index   24

What is an insect?

Insects are animals. All insects have a body made up of three parts and they all have three pairs of legs.

Most insects have wings and many of them have feelers on their heads. These feelers are called **antennae**.

Most insects are small, but in a place called Indonesia there is a stick insect that would fit across this open book!

The body of an insect

All insects have the same body plan.

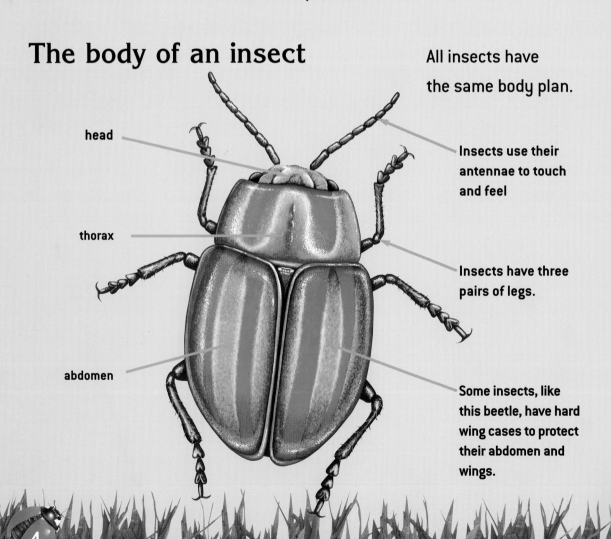

head

thorax

abdomen

Insects use their antennae to touch and feel

Insects have three pairs of legs.

Some insects, like this beetle, have hard wing cases to protect their abdomen and wings.

A hard case

We have bones inside our body called a skeleton.

Insects have no skeleton. They have a hard case on the outside of their bodies. This is called an **exoskeleton**. It protects their soft insides.

This shield bug has a very clear exoskeleton. It's just like a suit of armour.

DID YOU KNOW?

Insects were living on Earth long before the dinosaurs. Scientists know this because they have found fossils of insects in very old rocks.

A fossil of a dragonfly.

Insect families

There are more than one million different kinds of insects. Each kind is called a **species**. Scientists have sorted them into families.

Here are seven of the biggest families. Each family has something special about it.

Insect families

Beetle family
- Special feature: hard wing cases
- How many: more than 380,000 species

Butterfly and moth family
- Special feature: wings covered by tiny scales
- How many: about 140,000 species

Bee, wasp and ant family
- Special feature: front and back wings hook together
- How many: more than 100,000 species

DID YOU KNOW?

This man is a scientist. He goes all over the world to find out more about insects.

People who study insects are called **entomologists.**

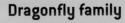

Fly family

- Special feature: only one pair of wings
- How many: about 65,000 species

Bug family

- Special feature: beak to stab and suck up food
- How many: about 60,000 species

Grasshopper and cricket family

- Special features: long body, leathery wings, strong back legs
- How many: about 20,000 species

Dragonfly family

- Special features: long body, two pairs of stiff wings
- How many: about 5,000 species

Wings

Most insects can fly. Flying helps them to find food and to escape from danger. Their wings are soft. If their wings get torn they can't be mended.

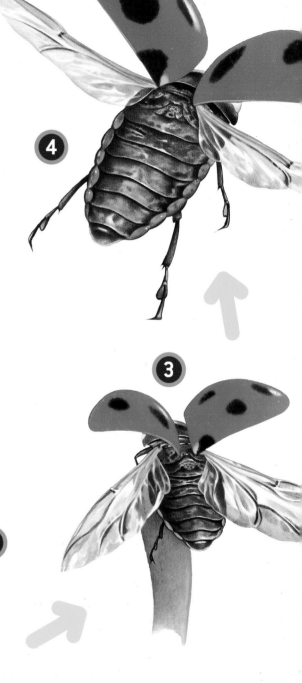

Flying

A ladybird is a kind of beetle. These pictures show a ladybird taking off.

1 The ladybird crawls to the top of a stem.

2 It opens its wing cases.

3 It unfolds its wings, and beats them up and down.

4 Soon the wings beat very quickly and lift the ladybird into the air.

Insect wings

A wasp has two pairs. The back pair is smaller than the front.

A butterfly has two pairs. The two pairs beat at the same time.

A dragonfly has two pairs. Each pair works on its own.

A house fly has only one pair of wings.

A butterfly's wings

Most insects have **transparent** wings. Butterfly wings are different – they have tiny scales that overlap like roof tiles.

DID YOU KNOW?

- Flies beat their wings up to 1,000 times every second. That's why they buzz!
- About 300 million years ago there were dragonflies as big as seagulls!

A close-up photo of the scales on a butterfly's wings.

Insect senses

When we want to know things we use our senses. We look, listen, smell, feel and taste.

Like us, insects use their senses. Mostly they use their eyes and **antennae**.

Looking around

Insects have very big **compound eyes**. These are made up of hundreds of little eyes called eye-lets.

All the little eye-lets make up a picture. This gives insects a very wide view, but they can't see as clearly as we can.

Compound eyes

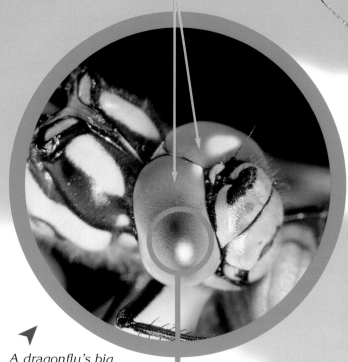

A dragonfly's big eyes take up most of its head

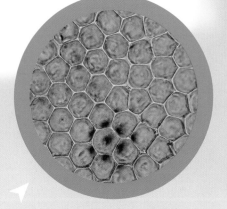

This close-up photo shows how the eye-lets fit together. Some insects have 15,000 eye-lets in each eye.

Antennae at work

Antennae are useful tools. Insects use them to touch, taste, smell and feel. Sometimes they even hear with them.

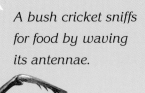

A bush cricket sniffs for food by waving its antennae.

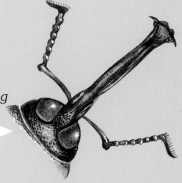

A weevil has antennae growing out of its snout.

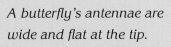

A butterfly's antennae are wide and flat at the tip.

A cockchafer beetle fans out its antennae to feel the wind.

DID YOU KNOW?

Dung beetles have an amazing sense of smell. It takes them just 60 seconds to find fresh dung!

Growing up

Insects lay tiny eggs. After they hatch, the young insects eat all the time.

As insects get bigger, they keep shedding their skin. Their bodies change shape. This is called **metamorphosis**. Some insects change quickly, but some take longer.

The life-cycle of a dragonfly

A dragonfly changes slowly.

2 In a few weeks each egg hatches into a **nymph**. It lives and feeds in the pond.

1 A dragonfly lays its eggs on a leaf near a pond.

3 Slowly the nymph grows bigger. Every time it sheds a skin, its wings are bigger. After two years, it turns into a dragonfly.

4 An adult dragonfly has full-size wings. It lives and feeds in the air.

shed skin

The life-cycle of a butterfly

A butterfly changes quickly.

2 After two weeks, the egg hatches into a caterpillar. It feeds on the plant and grows very fast.

1 A butterfly lays an egg on a plant.

3 One month later, the caterpillar makes a hard case called a **pupa**. Inside the pupa the caterpillar changes shape.

4 A few weeks later, a butterfly crawls out of the pupa and flies away.

Feeding

Some insects feed only on plants. Other insects feed only on animals.

They have different mouth parts because they eat different food.

Feeding on plants

Butterflies feed on the sweet nectar in flowers. Aphids make holes in stems and leaves and suck up the sap.

*A butterfly's long, curly tongue is called a **proboscis**. It sucks up nectar.*

proboscis

An aphid stabs plants with its beak and sucks up sap.

beak

Feeding on animals

Mosquitoes drink the blood of living animals. Some beetles feed off dead animals. They clean up all the waste.

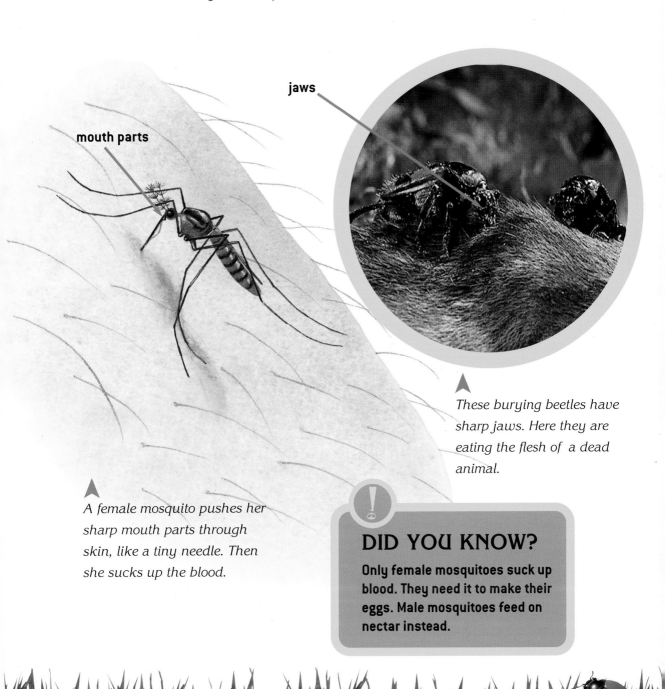

jaws

mouth parts

These burying beetles have sharp jaws. Here they are eating the flesh of a dead animal.

A female mosquito pushes her sharp mouth parts through skin, like a tiny needle. Then she sucks up the blood.

DID YOU KNOW?

Only female mosquitoes suck up blood. They need it to make their eggs. Male mosquitoes feed on nectar instead.

Staying alive

Insects have to do two things to stay alive. They have to find food and they have to protect themselves.

Hunting

Insects have different ways of hunting for food and catching **prey**.

*A flower mantis looks just like a flower. This is called **camouflage**. Other insects think it is a flower and land near it. Then the mantis eats them.*

The ant-lion larva hides in a sandy pit. It flicks sand at the ants. They fall down the pit and land in its jaws.

ant-lion larva

Enemies

Insects have many enemies. Spiders, frogs and birds often eat insects. Some insects try to hide. Some try to scare their enemies away.

A leaf insect hides using camouflage. It looks just like a leaf.

A bombardier beetle scares its enemies away. It makes a 'bang', and shoots out a hot spray that stings.

DID YOU KNOW?

The peacock butterfly has spots on its wings, like eyes. This scares its enemies.

Living together

Some insects live in large family groups called **colonies**. A colony is like a team. Every insect helps to make the nest, find food, fight enemies and look after the eggs and the young insects.

Ants, termites, wasps and bees all live in colonies.

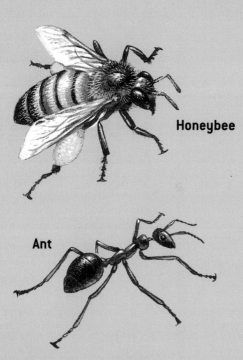
Honeybee

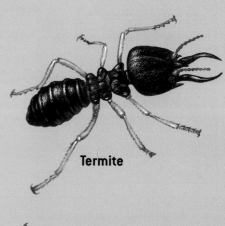
Termite

Ant

Wasp

A wasps' nest

Wasps build their nest out of thin sheets of paper. They make the paper by chewing up tiny bits of wood.

DID YOU KNOW?

A wasps' nest breaks easily. The wasps have to build a new one every year.
A bees' nest is much stronger. It is made of wax and can last for 50 years!

How wasps make a nest

1 The queen wasp starts the nest. She makes a small paper disc.

2 Next she makes little cups called cells and lays an egg in each one.

3 The eggs hatch and the young wasps grow fast. They grow into worker wasps. They make the nest bigger with lots of new cells.

4 As more and more wasps hatch, the nest gets bigger and bigger. In four months it is the size of a football and it has 10,000 tiny cells inside.

The inside of a wasps' nest

Insects in the home

Insects like to live in people's warm, dry houses. Most of them are so tiny that we can't even see them.

The housefly

Houseflies spread germs. They carry dirt from place to place on their legs. When they land on food, they vomit onto it. This makes the food runny, then the fly sucks it up.

The furniture beetle

The furniture beetle lays eggs that turn into tiny woodworms. They eat all kinds of wood. They can even make a wooden house fall down!

The flea

Fleas feed on the blood of animals like cats and dogs. They feed on humans only if they are very hungry.

The headlouse

Headlice live and lay their eggs in human hair. They are hard to get rid of because they have strong claws to hold on tight.

The dust mite

There are millions of dust mites in our homes. They eat the tiny flakes of dead skin that fall off our bodies every day.

Glossary

abdomen the back part of an insect's body

antennae the pair of feelers on an insect's head, which it uses to pick up messages

camouflage marks on an animal that help it blend into the background

colony lots of insects living together

compound eye an eye made up of many tiny eyes

entomologist someone who studies insects

exoskeleton the hard case on the outside of an insect's body

metamorphosis how insects change as they grow up

nymph a young insect that grows slowly but does not make a pupa

prey an animal that is hunted by another animal for food

proboscis a long tube to suck up nectar

pupa the hard case that some young insects make before they turn into an adult

species a group of animals that are all the same kind and can breed together

thorax the middle part of an insect's body

transparent so thin that you can see through it

Index

abdomen 4, 22
ant 6, 16, 18
antennae 4, 10–11, 22
ant-lion 16
aphid 14

bee 6, 18
  honeybee 18
beetle 4, 6, 8
  bombardier 17
  burying 15
  cockchafer 11
  dung 11
  furniture 20
bug 7
  shield 5
butterfly 6, 9, 11, 13, 14
  peacock 17

caterpillar 13
cricket 7
  bush 11

dragonfly 5, 7, 9, 10, 12
dust mite 21

entomologist 7, 22
exoskeleton 5, 22

eye 10

flea 21
flower mantis 16
fly 7, 9, 20
  house 9, 20

grasshopper 7

headlouse 21

ladybird 8
leaf insect 17

metamorphosis 12, 22
mosquito 15
moth 6

nymph 12, 23

pupa 13, 23

stick insect 4

termite 18
thorax 4, 23

wasp 6, 9, 18, 19
weevil 11
wing 4, 5–9, 12, 17